My PRACTISING PHOTOGRAPHY

PARIS MEHARG

Copyright © 2024 by Paris Meharg. 857991

All rights reserved. No part of this book may be reproduced or transmitted in any form or by any means, electronic or mechanical, including photocopying, recording, or by any information storage and retrieval system, without permission in writing from the copyright owner.

To order additional copies of this book, contact:
Xlibris
AU TFN: 1 800 844 927 (Toll Free inside Australia)
AU Local: 02 8310 8187 (+61 2 8310 8187 from outside Australia)
www.xlibris.com.au
Orders@Xlibris.com.au

ISBN:	Softcover	979-8-3694-9613-8
	EBook	979-8-3694-9612-1

Library of Congress Control Number: 2024907599

Print information available on the last page

Rev. date: 04/12/2024

My name is Paris Lee Meharg

I am a twin we where born 17/10/02

I've always wanted to be a photographer since the age of ten years old here is a few of my photos I took but sadly the publisher won't let me put no more photos in my book I was lied to about how many photos can go in my book 🙁 I am happy to do cheap photos for anyone willing to pay and if you want me to travel you will have to pay for me to go to you and home again as I don't drive and you will have to understand I don't travel alone I will have either mum or a friend travel with me.

Thanking you your practising photographer
Paris

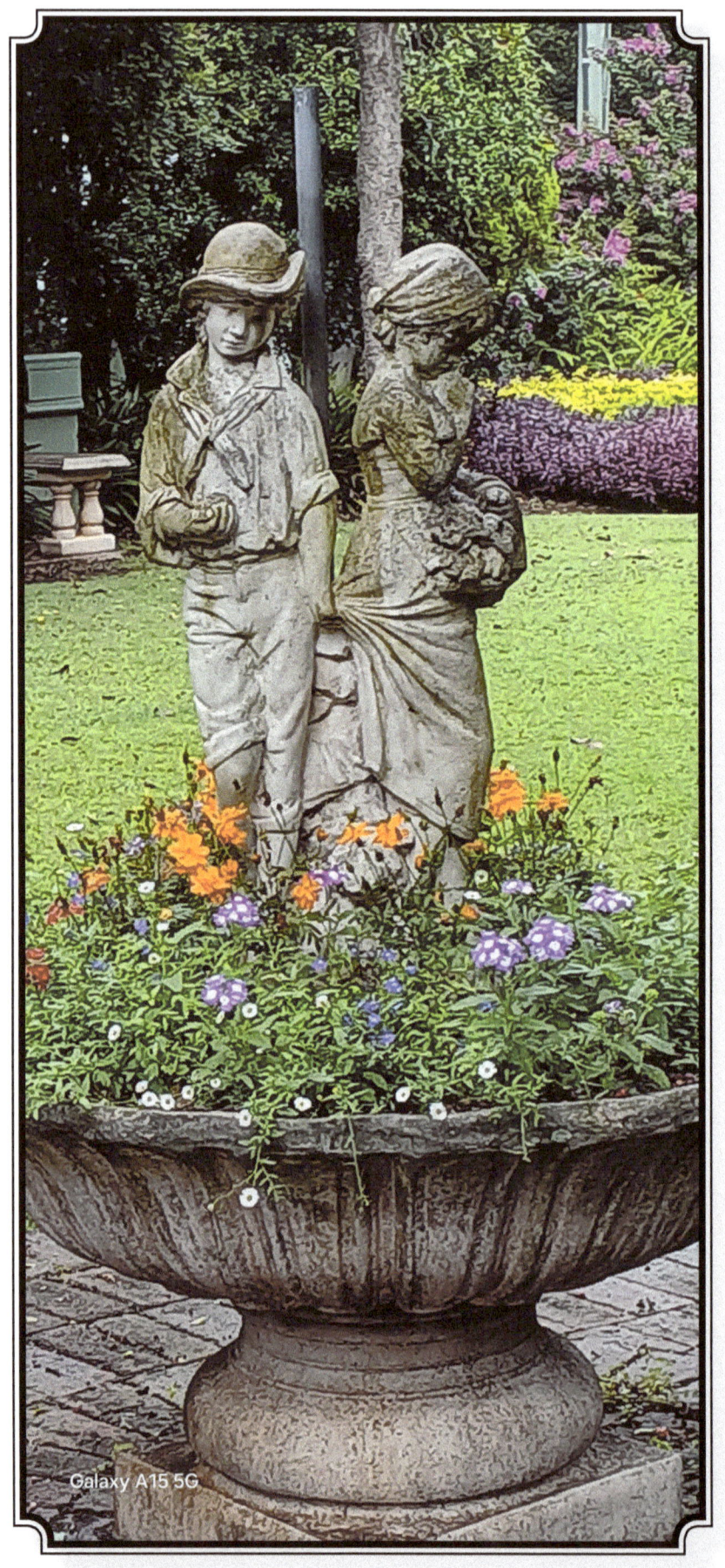

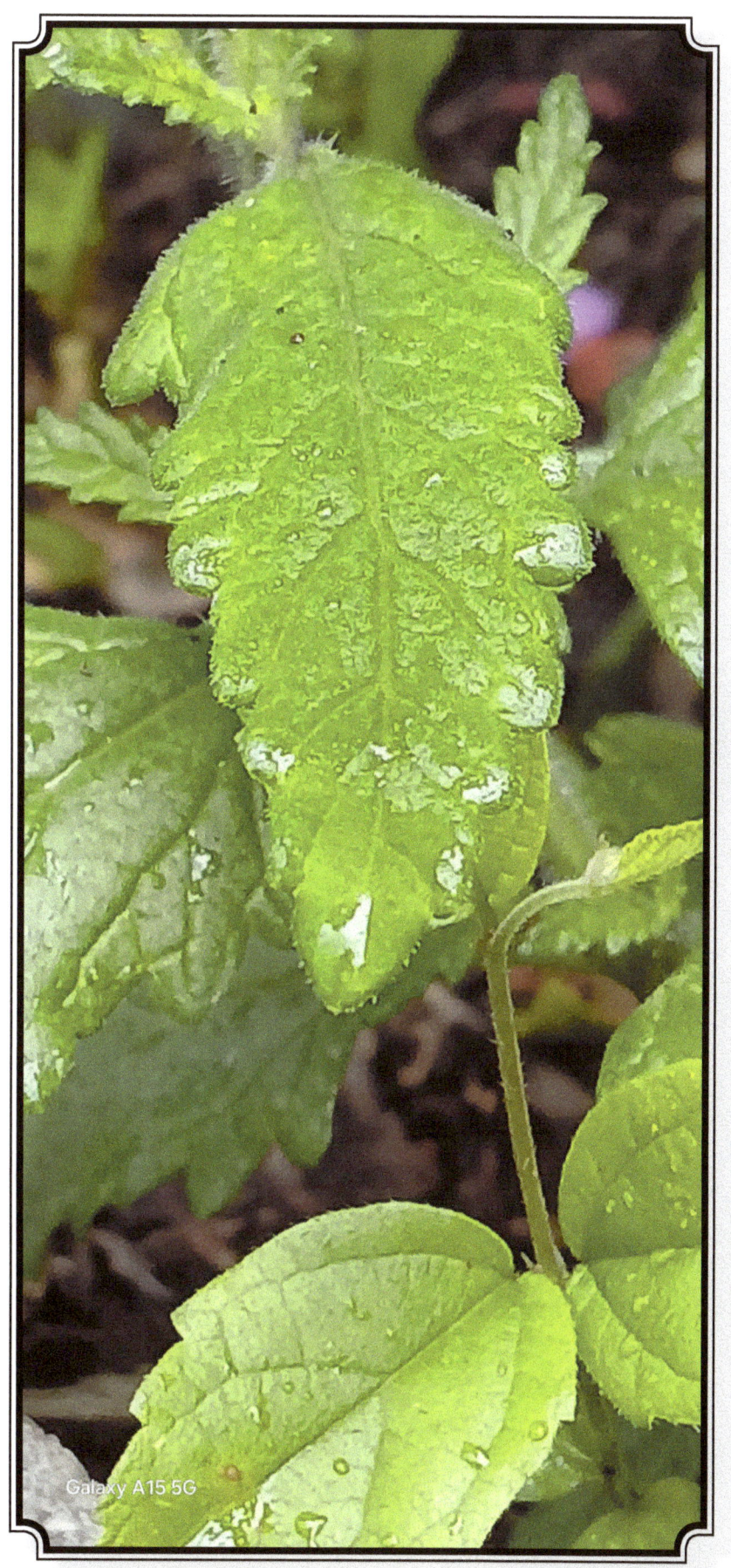

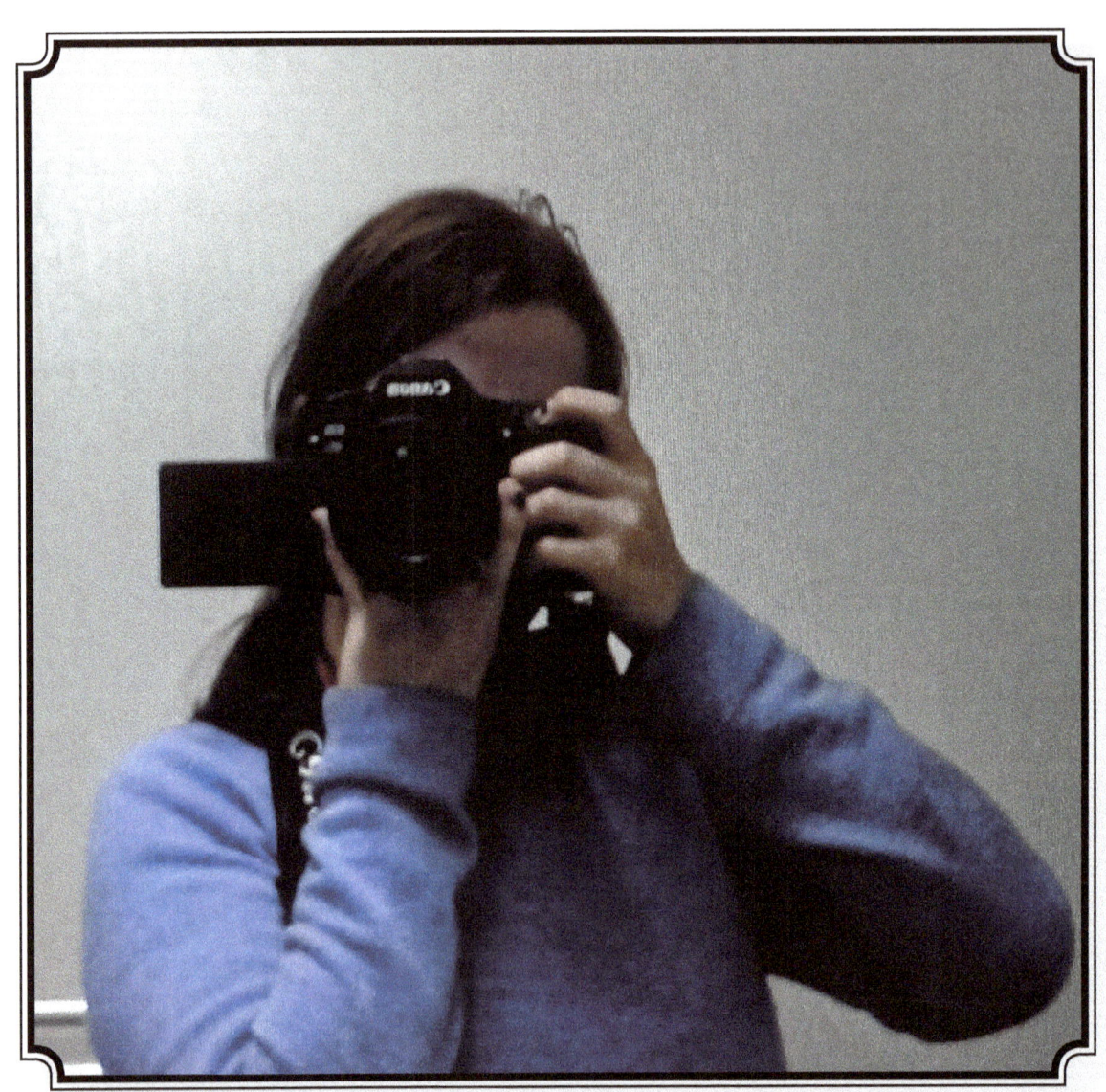

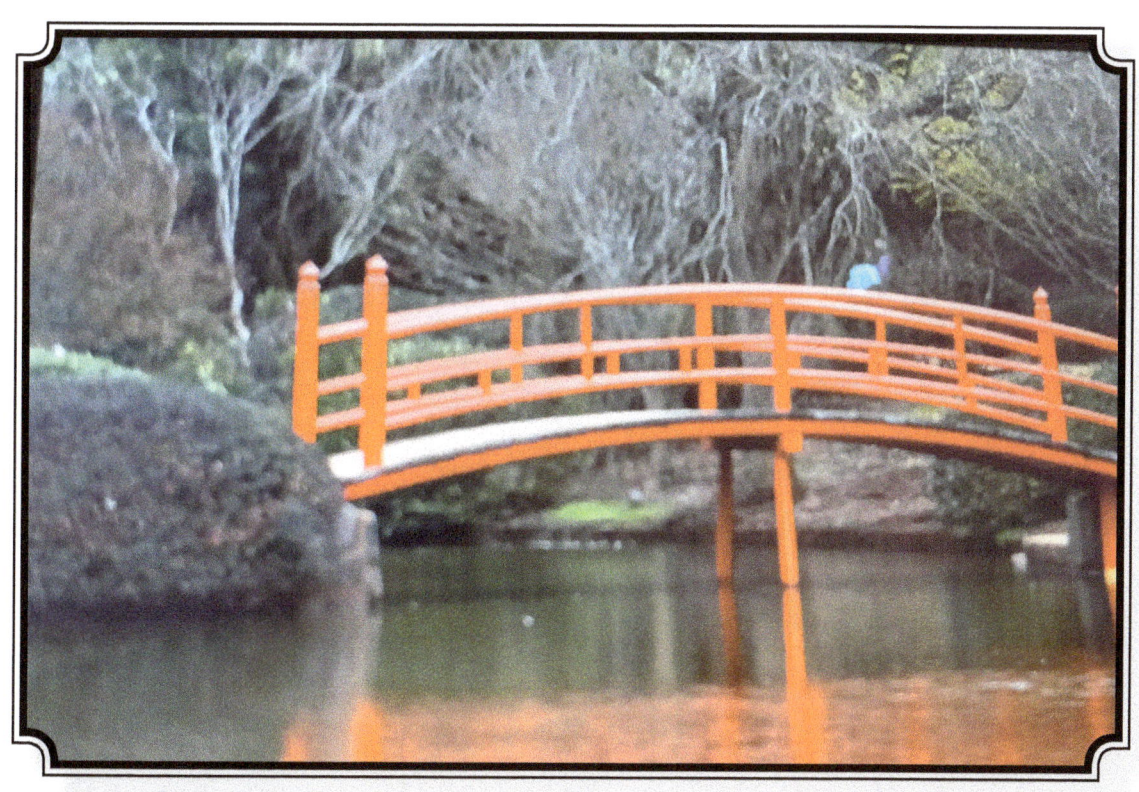

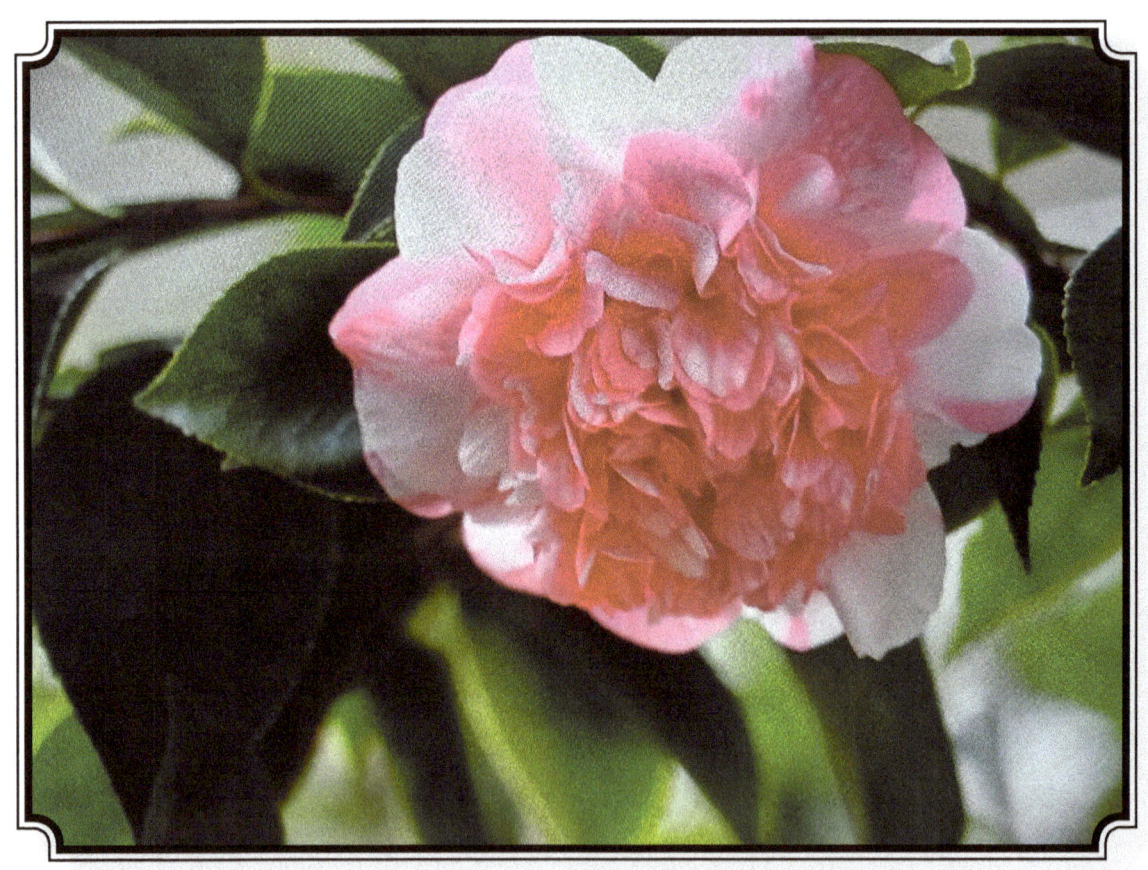

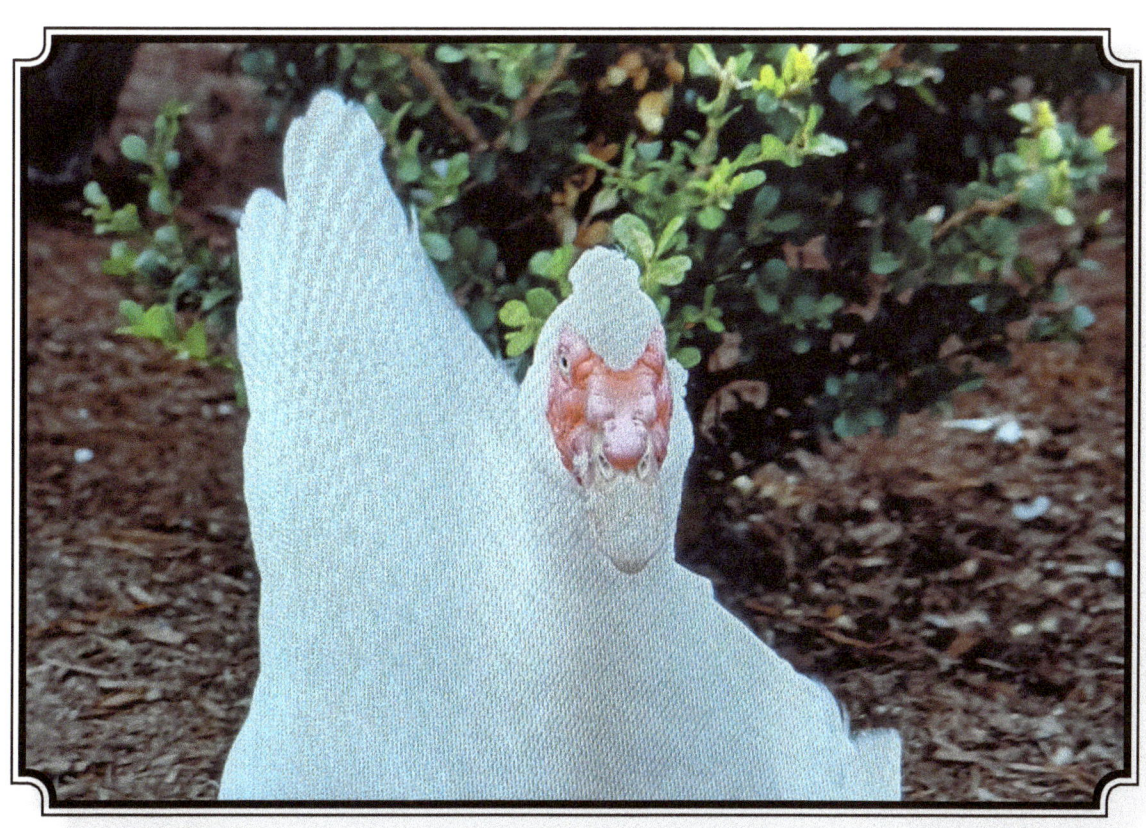

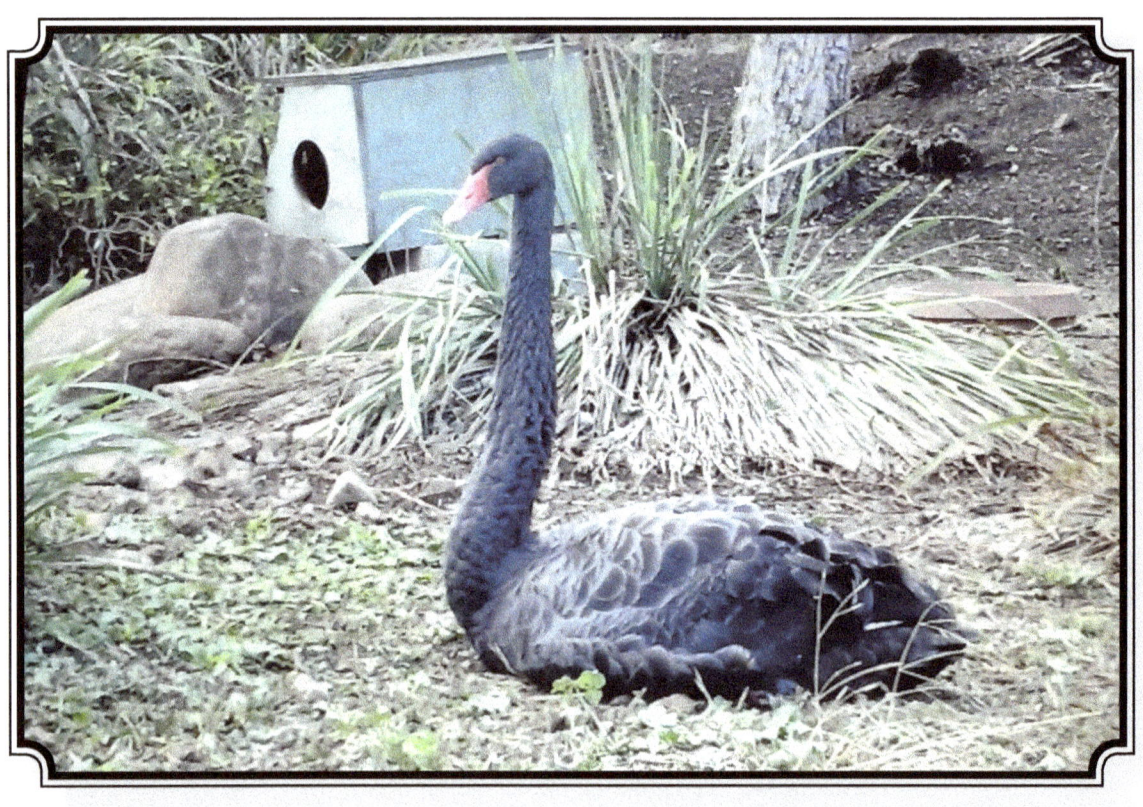

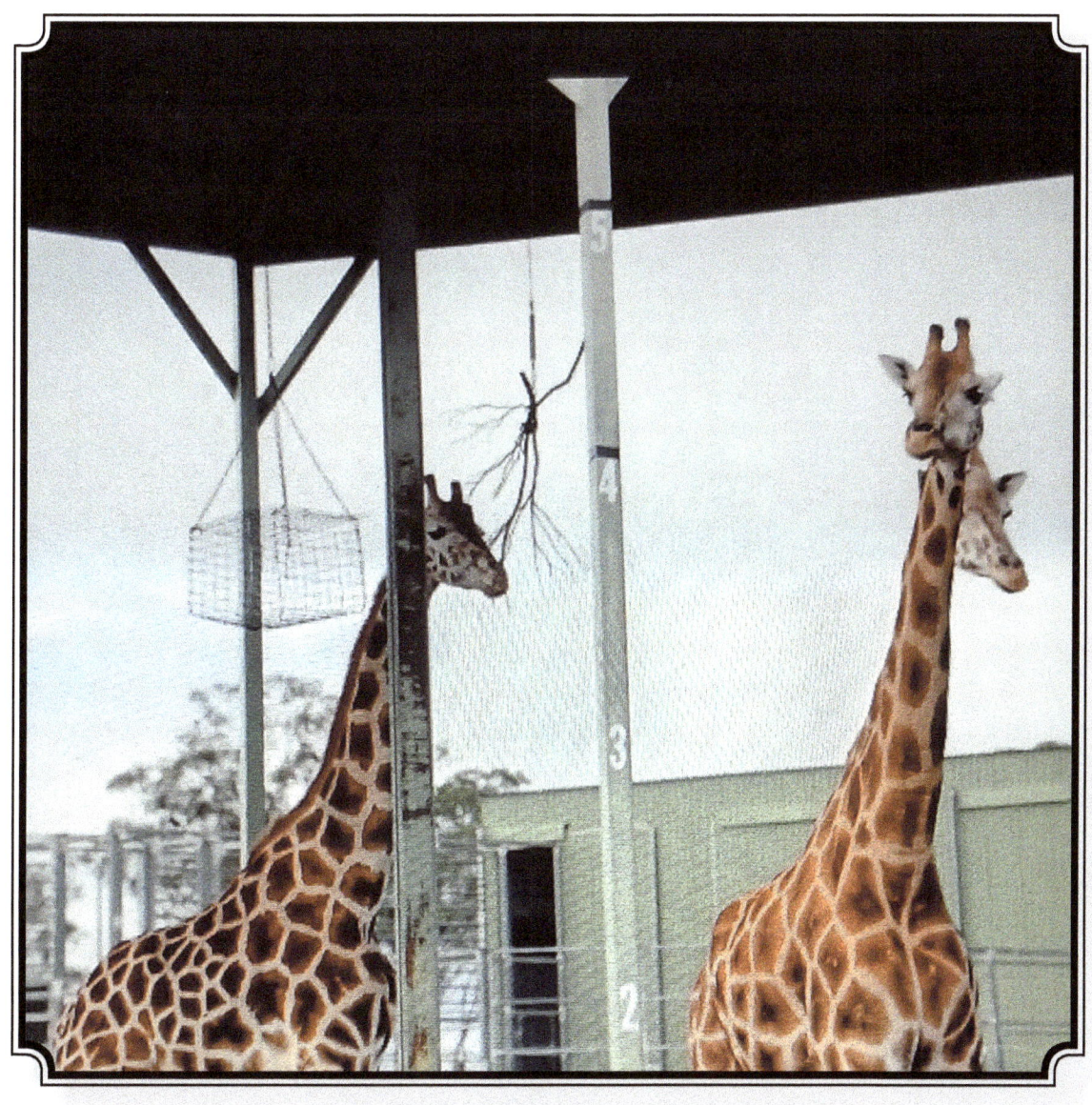

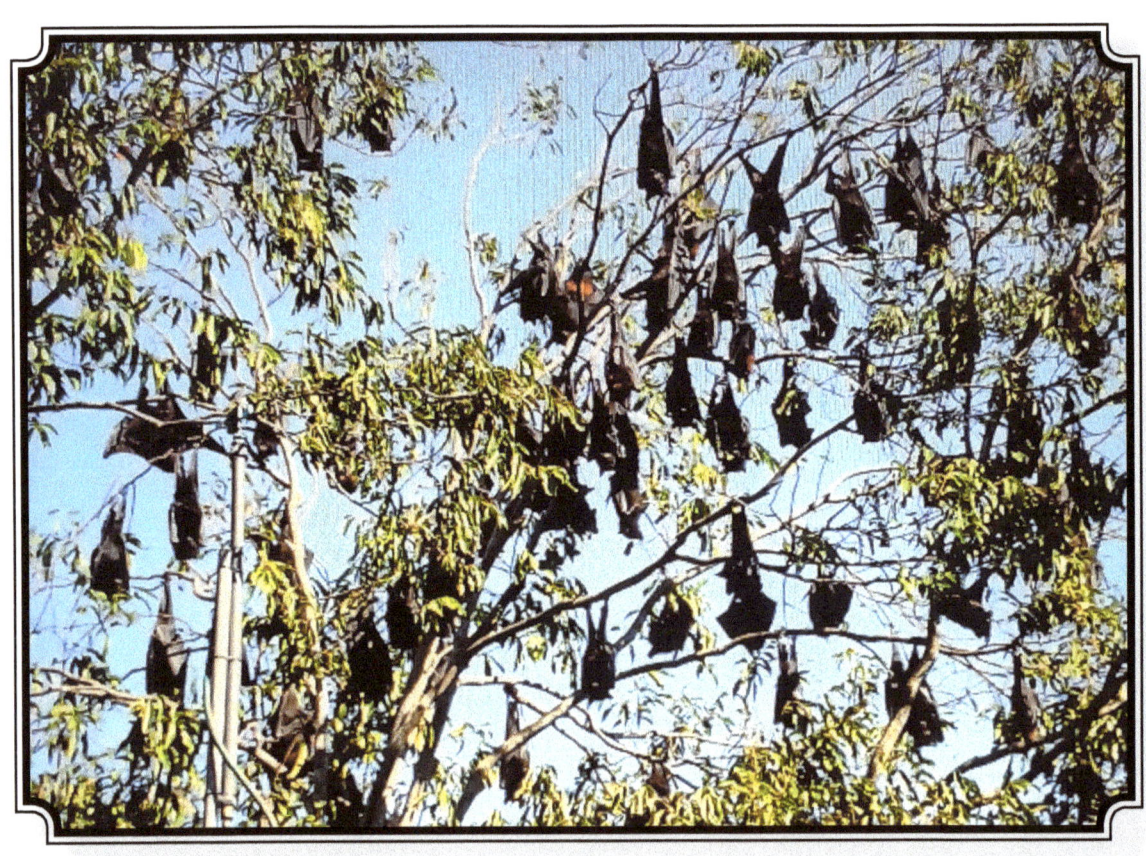

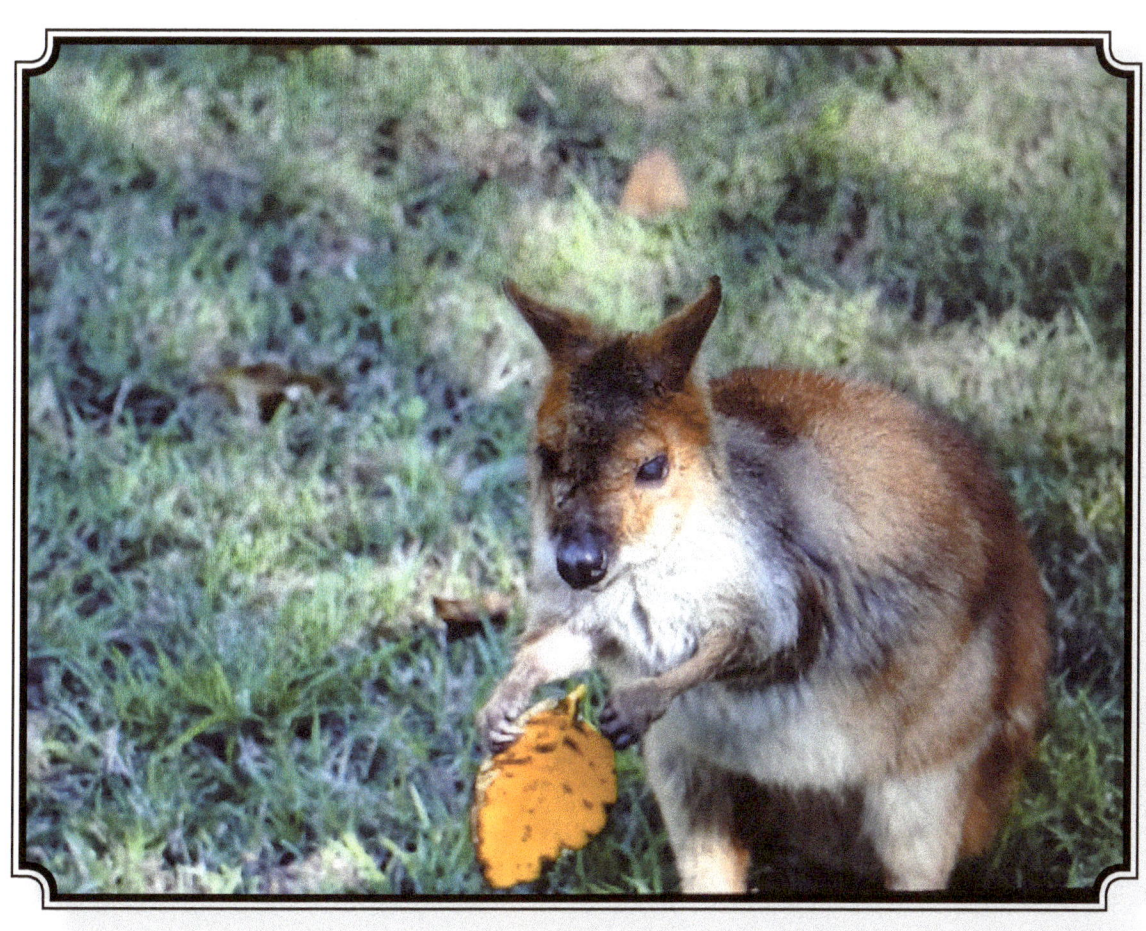

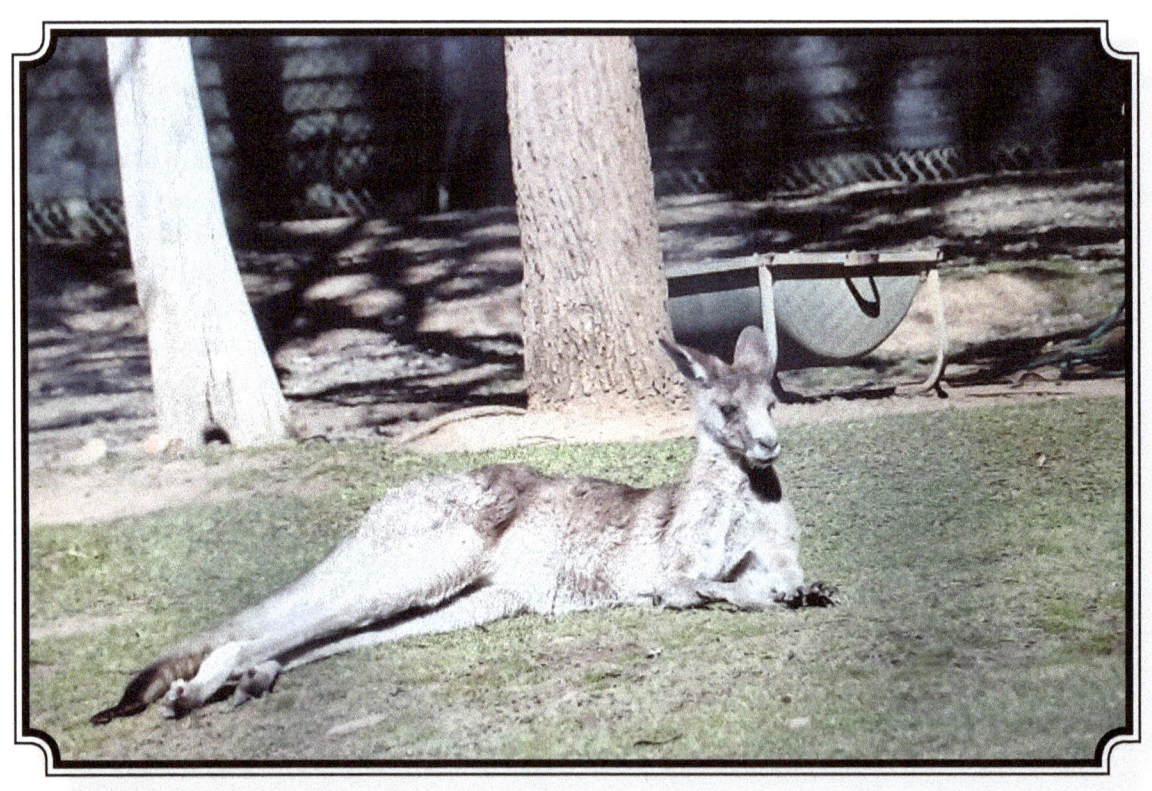

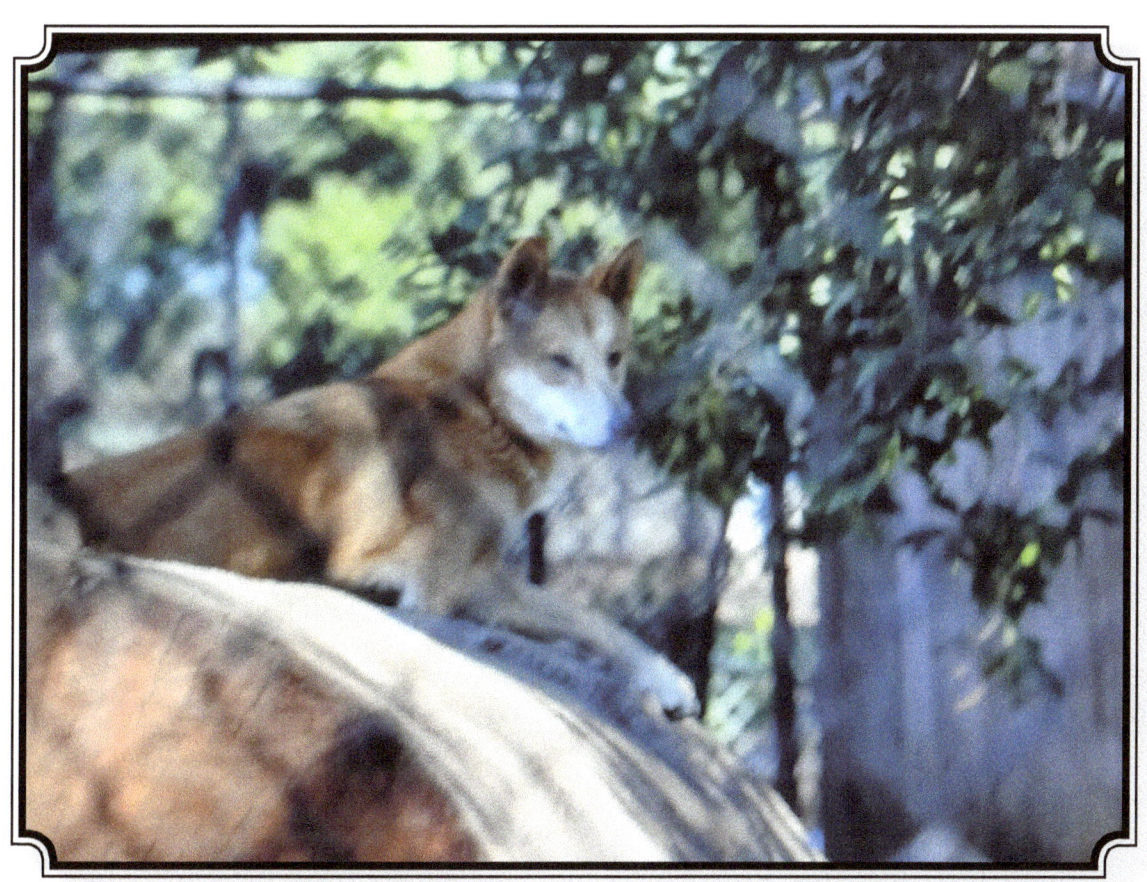

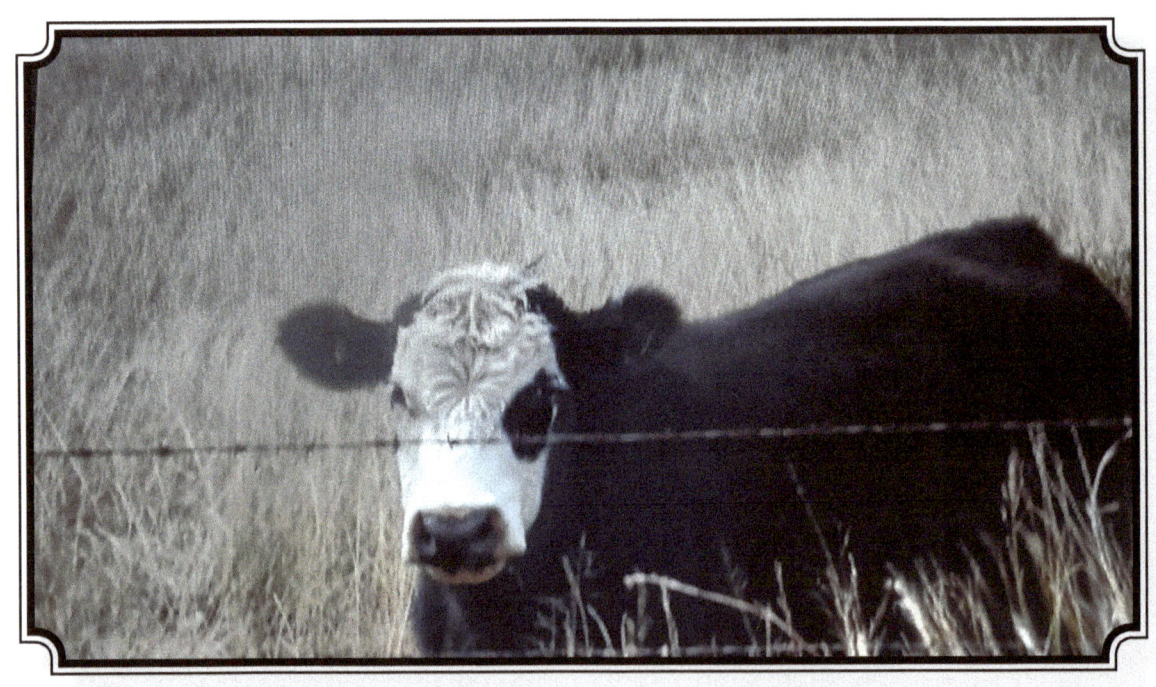

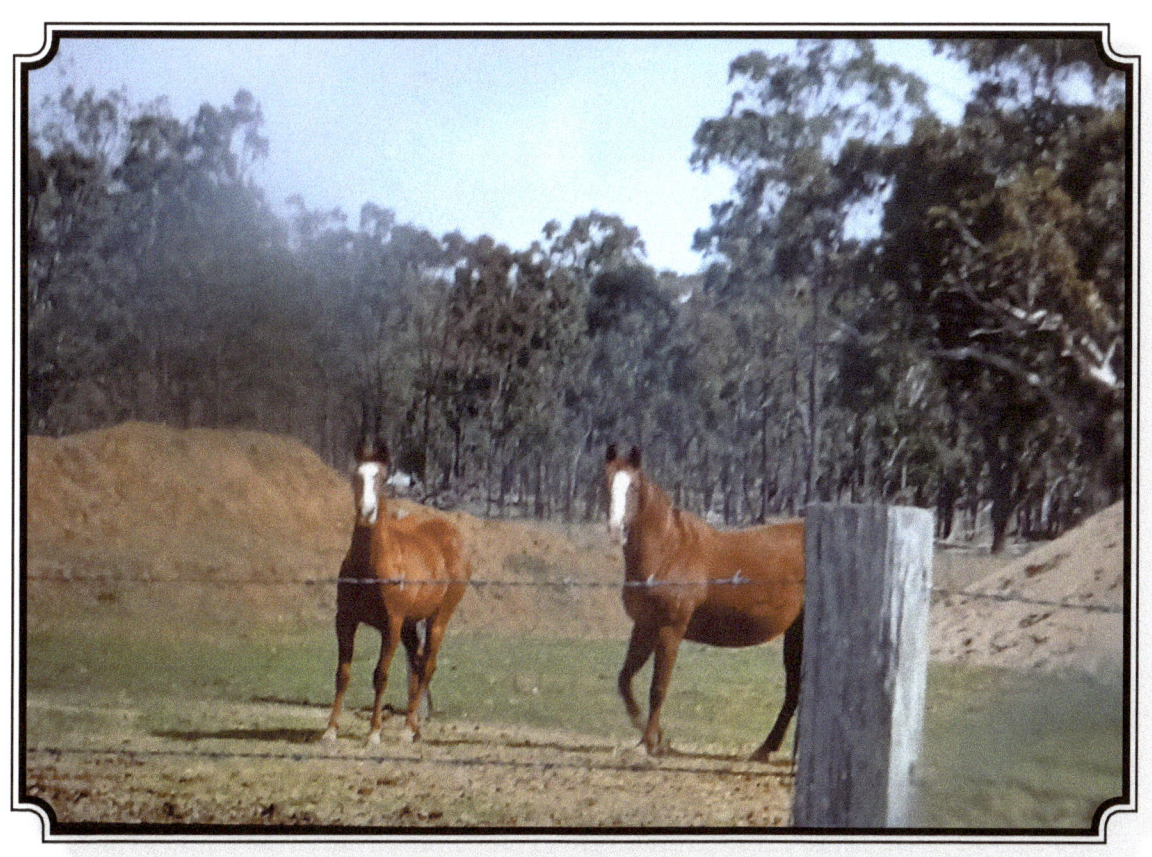

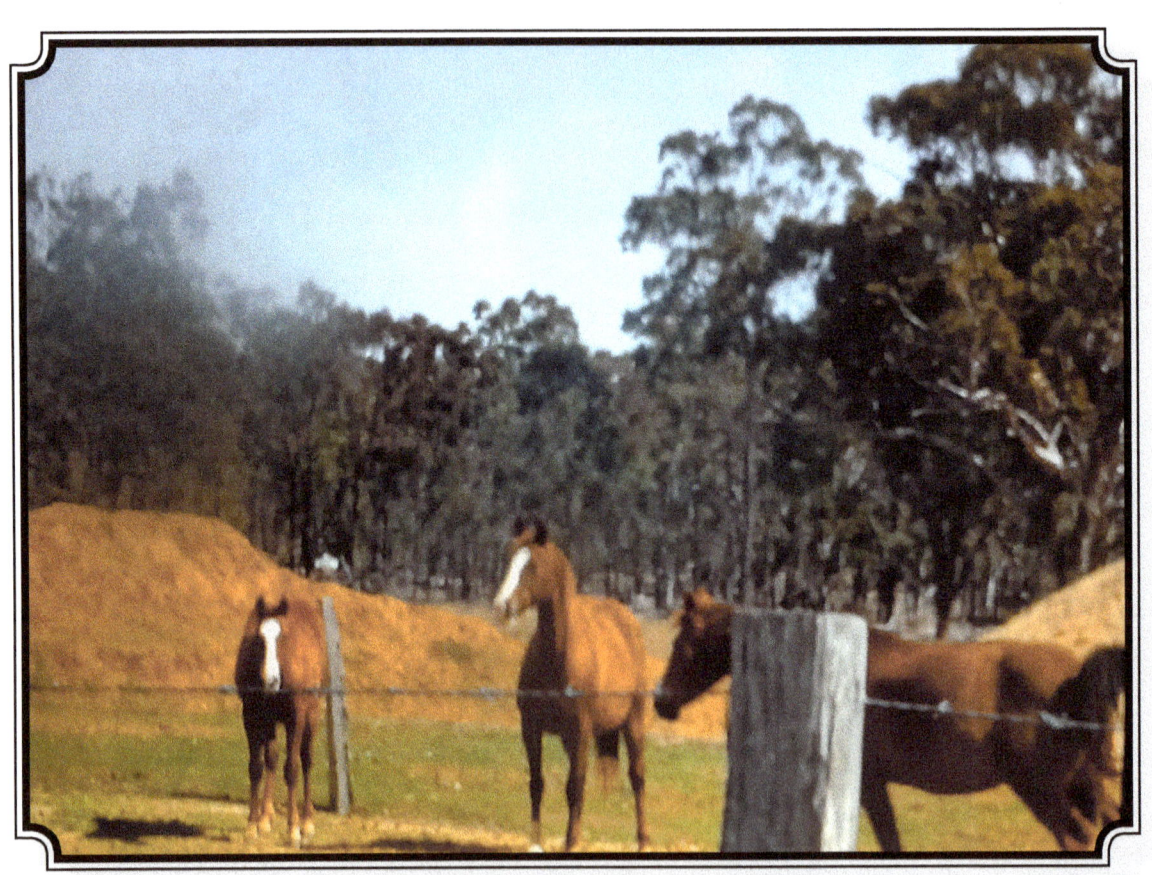

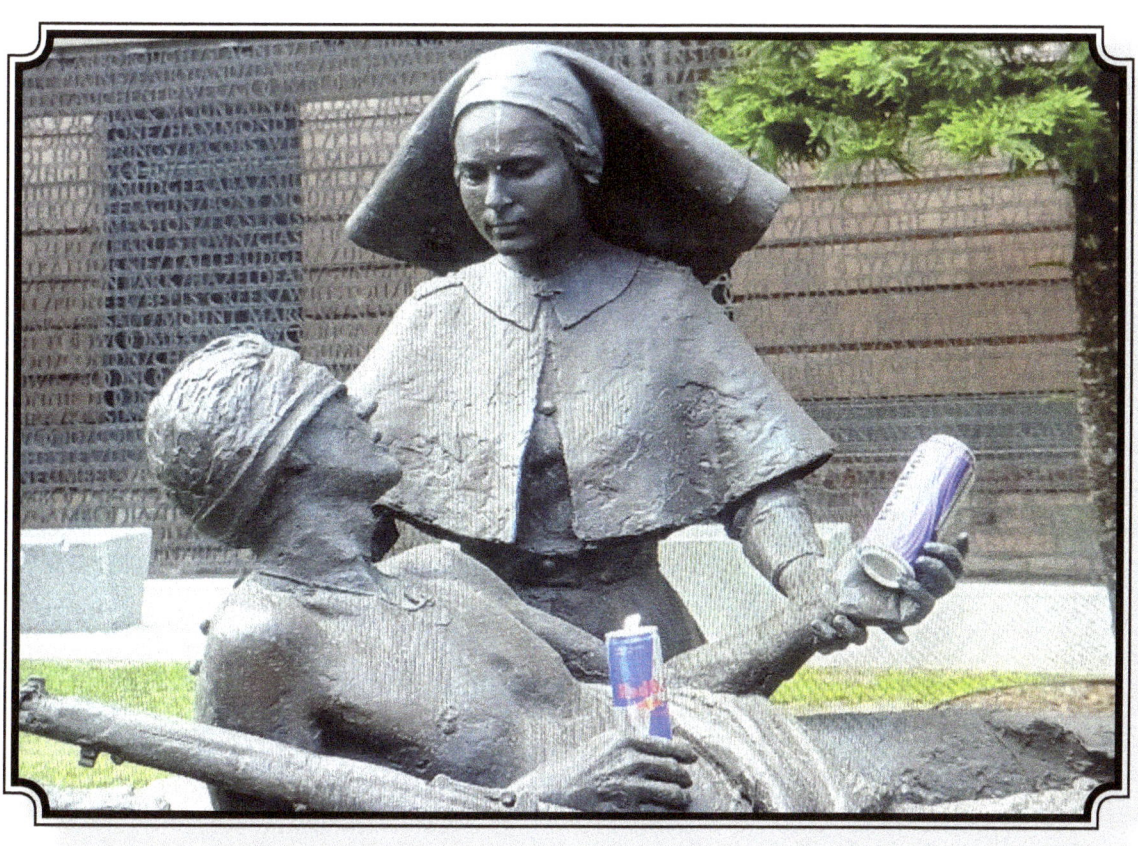

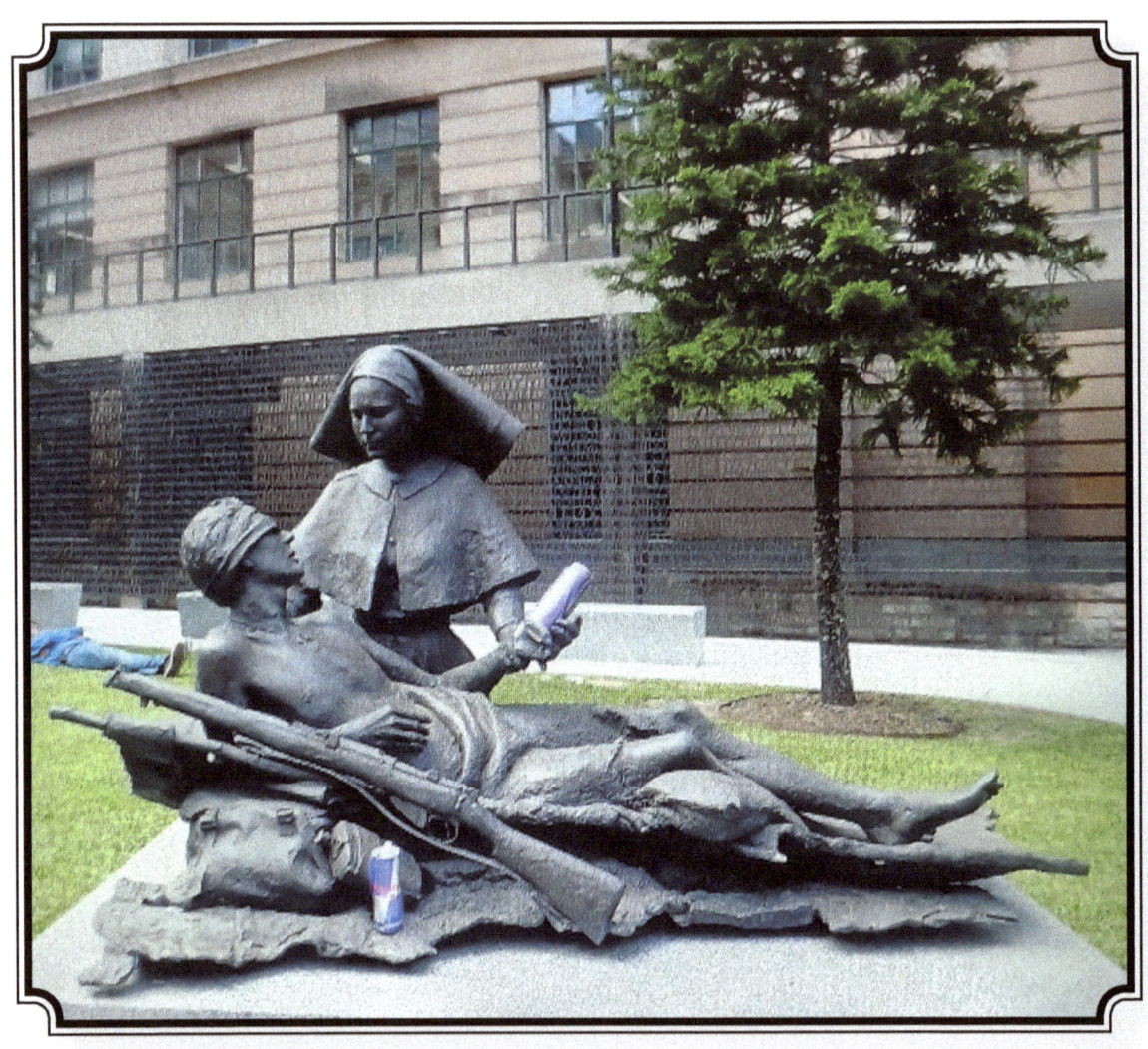

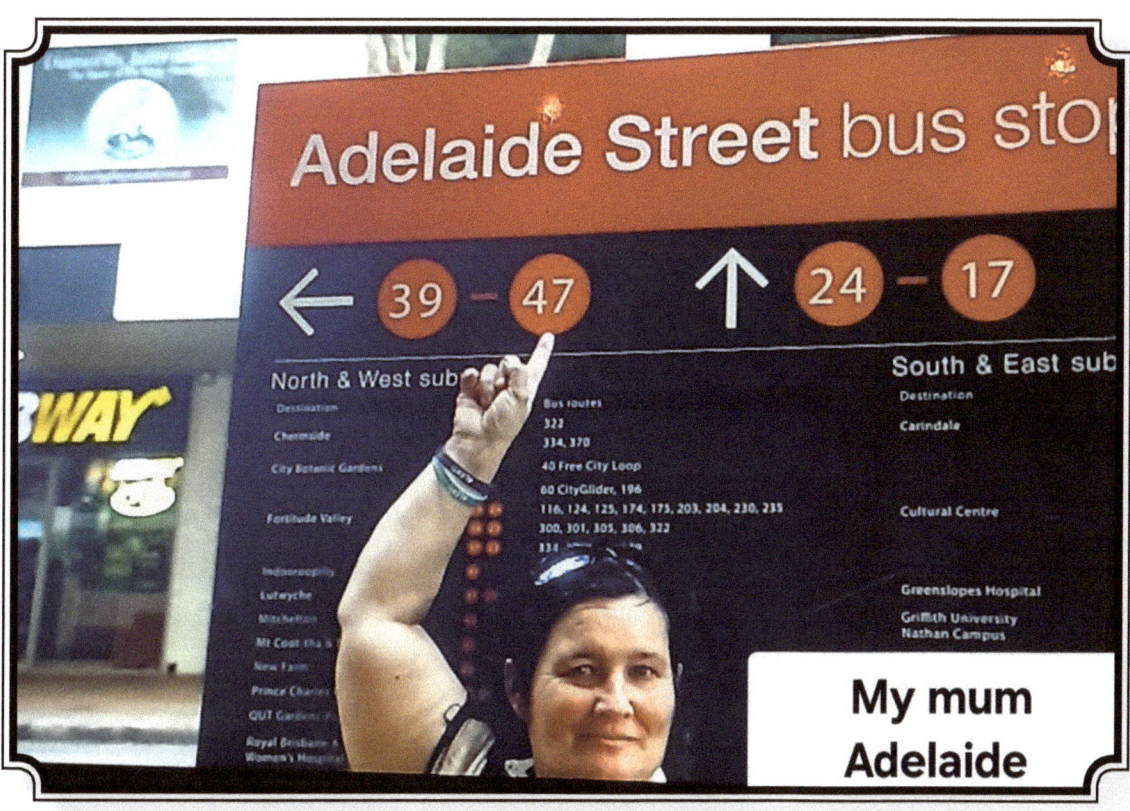

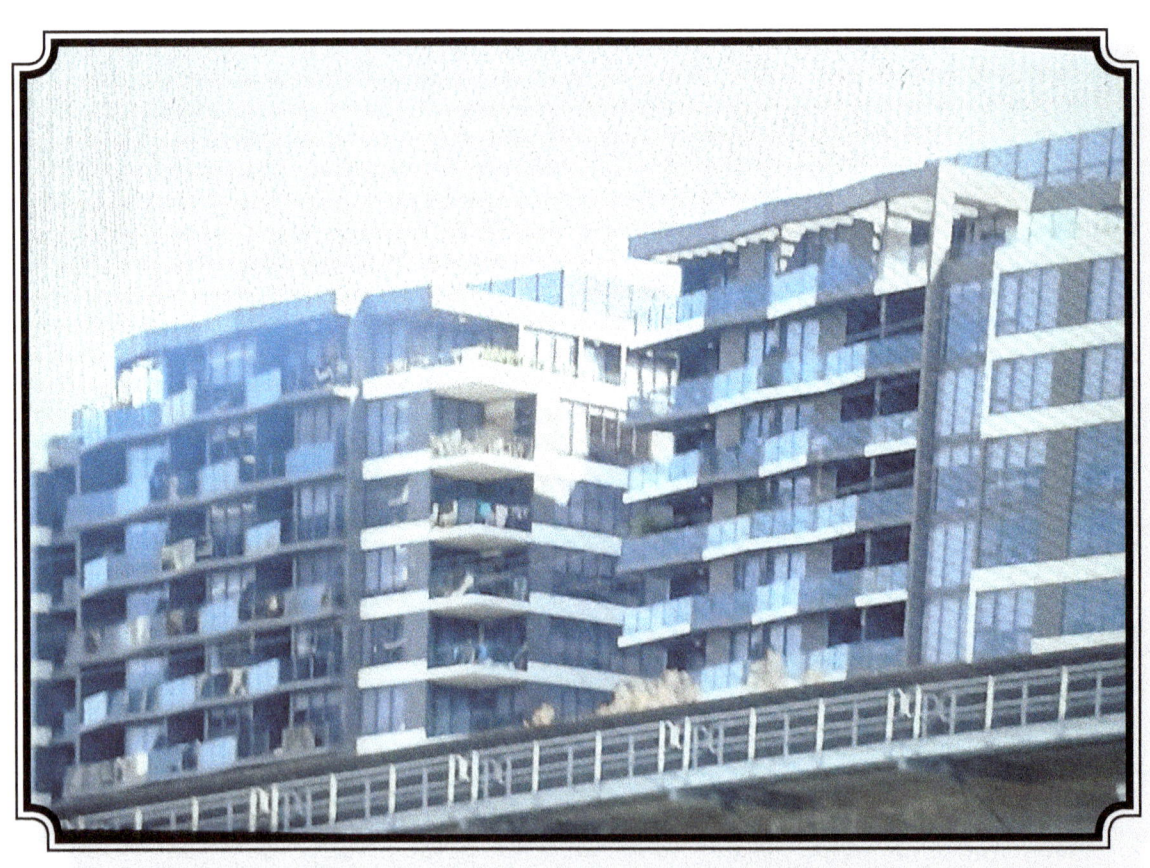

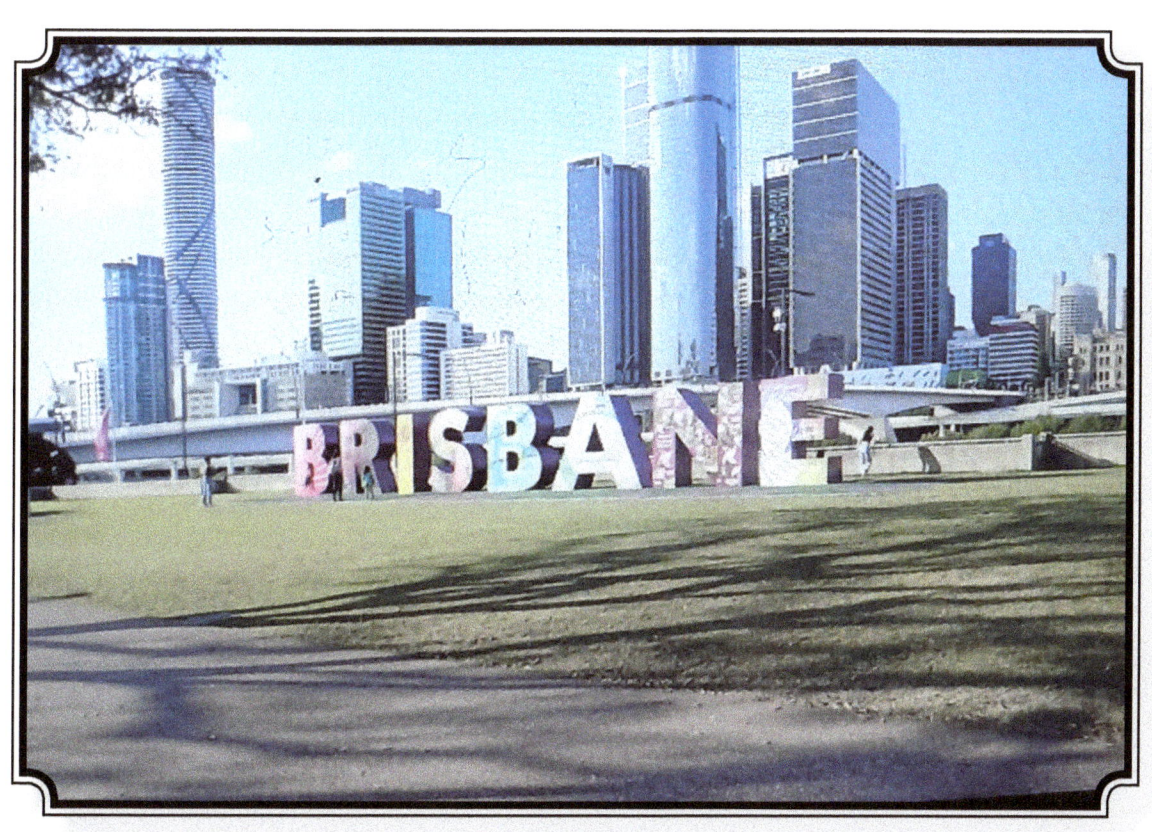

www.ingramcontent.com/pod-product-compliance
Lightning Source LLC
Chambersburg PA
CBHW040545220526
45473CB00016B/3028